D0831310

IT'S NOT WHAT YOU SAY
How to Sell Your Message
When It Matters Most

MICHAEL PARKER

A PERIGEE BOOK

PERIGEE
An imprint of Penguin Random House LLC
375 Hudson Street, New York, New York 10014

IT'S NOT WHAT YOU SAY

ISBN: 978-0-399-17543-5

First American edition: December 2015
Previously published in Great Britain in 2014 by Vermilion, an imprint of Ebury Publishing.

PRINTED IN THE UNITED STATES OF AMERICA

3   5   7   9   10   8   6   4   2

While the author has made every effort to provide accurate telephone numbers and Internet addresses at the time of publication, neither the publisher nor the author assumes any responsibility for errors, or for changes that occur after publication. Further, publisher does not have any control over and does not assume any responsibility for author or third-party websites or their content.

Most Perigee books are available at special quantity discounts for bulk purchases for sales promotions, premiums, fund-raising, or educational use. Special books, or book excerpts, can also be created to fit specific needs. For details, write: SpecialMarkets@penguinrandomhouse.com.

AUDITIONS
£undrai$ing
Lecturing
INTERVIEWING
PUBLIC SPEAKING
Debating

Pitching

Persuading

Performing

PRESENTING

proposing

Preaching

Negotiating

To Eliza

CONTENTS

PRINCIPLES.

PREPARATION.

PITCH.

PERFORMANCE.

PERFECT.

PRINC

IPLES.

"THOSE ARE
MY PRINCIPLES,
AND IF YOU
DON'T LIKE
THEM . . . WELL,
I HAVE OTHERS."

GROUCHO MARX

IT'S NOT WHAT YOU SAY . . .

When faced with the spotlight, most of us tend to focus on the content—the *what* we say—at the expense of the delivery—the *way* we say it. This is the difference between mediocre speakers and great ones.

The impact of your words on an audience comes mainly from your tone of voice and body language. Although this cannot be measured precisely, a fascinating study carried out in the United States by the National Security Agency demonstrated the importance of delivery.

Three research groups were asked to judge if suspects were telling the truth in 300 criminal cases that had known outcomes. One group only listened to the interviews, and were 55% right. Another group saw them but without any sound, and were 65% right, while those who saw *and* heard them scored 85%.

Martin Luther King Jr.'s speeches were eloquent enough in their written form, but inspiration leaps when we hear and see his performance of his famous "I have a dream" speech—the words become spine tingling.

"I would not hesitate to assert that a mediocre speech supported by all the power of delivery will be more impressive than the best speech unaccompanied by such power." **QUINTILIAN, *INSTITUTES OF ORATORY***

PEOPLE BUY PEOPLE

Whether you are interviewing, auditioning or making a speech, there is one thing performances have in common: you are being judged. It might be by an audience, by a panel or—in some ways more scarily—by your own friends and colleagues.

When preparing for the big moment, you are likely to put everything into crafting your speech, polishing your résumé and practicing your technique, but you might well forget the essential rule learned by the early traveling salesmen. They knew that before they could sell their encyclopedias, they had to sell *themselves.*

"Character may almost be called the most effective means of persuasion." ARISTOTLE

IF THEY DON'T LIKE YOU, THEY WON'T BUY YOU

An obvious statement, but often overlooked. Your qualifications may be exceptional, or your cause undeniably deserving, but if they don't like you they won't buy you.

Fortunately, most of us, most of the time, are likable when among friends and when things are going well. We are less likable when we feel stressed or uncertain—feelings that are heightened whenever we are in the spotlight.

You can counter this, and keep your natural likability, by being prepared and rehearsed.

Rehearsal makes nice people nicer!

Nelson Mandela cultivated his likable image through every aspect of his appearance, not least his beatific smile.

PEOPLE ACT ON EMOTION, THEN JUSTIFY WITH REASON

The human mind is often thought of as divided into two parts: emotional and rational.

We understand the active power of emotion: how we often react from fear, act out of love or greed, or do things against our better judgment. We understand this, and yet, when faced with an audience, we tend to focus our *minds*—not our hearts—on persuasion that assumes a rational response. We hone arguments, revise scripts and fine-tune to the last minute. Emotion gets sidelined.

We ignore the advice of the legendary Dale Carnegie, who told us in his seminal book *How to Win Friends and Influence People*:

"When dealing with people, let us remember we are not dealing with creatures of logic. We are dealing with creatures of emotion, creatures bristling with prejudices and motivated by pride and vanity."

We forget that emotion leads to action, whereas reason just leads to conclusions. We forget about feelings.

"I've learned that people will forget what you said, people will forget what you did, but people will never forget how you made them feel." **MAYA ANGELOU**

PASSION PERSUADES

One definition of passion is "an intense and compelling emotion."
If you are genuinely passionate about your subject, you are already
halfway to being able to persuade.

Passion is infectious, so let it out. Don't hold back. With it, you
can be unstoppable.

However, there will inevitably be occasions where you do not feel passion.
In which case, don't claim it. This will seem false.

When passion is not a reality, enthusiasm, interest and eagerness are all powerful motivations for you and for your audience, so work on them.

But if you can, find passion.

"Probably my worst quality is that I get very passionate about what I think is right." **HILLARY CLINTON**

"HUNGER IS THE BEST SAUCE."

16TH-CENTURY PROVERB

Choosing from similarly excellent, deserving candidates or pitches isn't easy. The proposals may be compelling and the arguments persuasive, but the real decision will usually come down to the judges' sense of **who is the hungriest.**

Hunger is not something you proclaim. You ooze it by being hell-bent, doing more, asking more, leaving no proverbial stone unturned. A world-famous actress was hungry when pitching her film *Unbroken*:

"This has been the hardest thing I have ever done. I had all these hours of phone calls and things and made all these boards. I took my glue and tape and pictures off the Internet . . . I put all my boards in a garbage bag and I carried them to Universal myself and put them out, and I pitched my butt off."
ANGELINA JOLIE

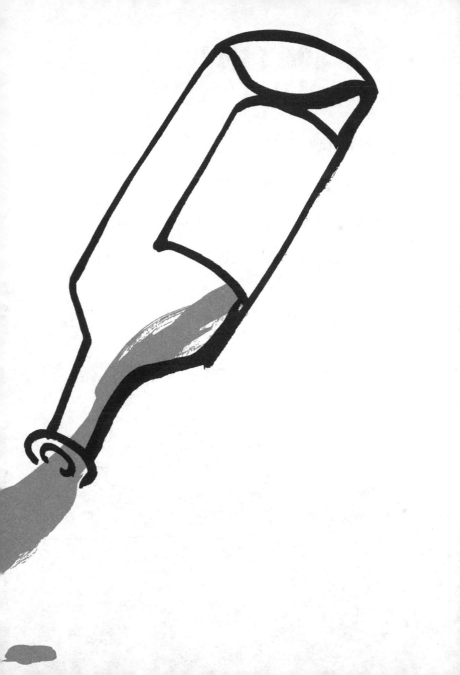

IF YOU DON'T LEAD, NO ONE WILL FOLLOW

Every pitch is a battle.

A battle against time, against rivals.

And every pitch takes energy, preparation and performance.

Clear-cut victories are rare. Often the winning difference, as on a real field of battle, is leadership.

On your own or heading a team, take charge.
Be bold. Be inspirational. Be courageous.

"When placed in command, take charge."
**GENERAL "STORMIN'" NORMAN
SCHWARZKOPF**

MAKE THE AUDIENCE
YOUR FRIEND

The audience is not your enemy.

When you're in the spotlight, particularly for the first time, it's easy to think your audience is against you—a disembodied group just waiting for you to slip up. This is not the case!

They are not there under sufferance. Generally, they are there because they want to be there; they are looking forward to meeting you and being part of an engaging experience.

It's not *you* against *them.* They bring interest and energy for you to tap into, sharing the moment with you.

Even though you're the one talking, think of your presentation as the beginning of a lively conversation among friends.

"Do I not destroy my enemies when I make them my friends?"
ABRAHAM LINCOLN

IT'S *ALL* ABOUT THE EMOTIONAL CONNECTION

Your proposal was bulletproof.

Your interview was flawless.

Your lecture was illuminating.

Your speech was profound.

BUT ...

Did you make an emotional connection?

THE FIVE CANONS OF RHETORIC

Rhetoric can be defined as the art of persuasion, influencing with words rather than force. Arguably the greatest masters of this art were ancient writers Aristotle, Cicero and Quintilian. And it was Quintilian, the Roman rhetorician from Spain, who said:

"The whole art of oratory, as the most and greatest writers have taught, consists of five parts: invention, arrangement, style, memory and delivery."

Each of these elements is as valuable today in creating effective communication as when it was first taught over 2,000 years ago.

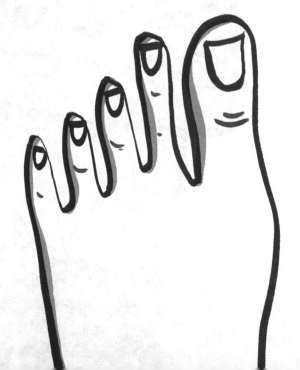

1. *INVENTIO* (invention)

This is the stage of exploring all the possible avenues of what
you might say about your subject, keeping the interests of your audience
in mind.

From the Latin, *invenire* (to come upon) and the Greek *heuristic*
(to discover), this phase calls for research and imagination.

The goal is to find an idea that will be the framework of all that follows—
an idea that provokes a:

Eureka!

2. *DISPOSITIO* (arrangement)

This is the process of organizing your arguments for maximum impact. In Greek, the word is *taxis*—to arrange troops for battle.

There are six main parts of a speech:

i. **Exordium,** *"to prepare the audience in such a way that they will be disposed to lend a ready ear to the rest of the speech."* (Quintilian)

ii. **Narration,** where you set out your issue or your proposition.

iii. **Partition,** where you summarize the arguments you are about to make. (You're telling the audience what to expect, making it easier to follow.)

iv. **Proof,** the arguments in full.

v. **Refutation,** the destruction of any opposing arguments.

vi. **Peroration,** a summary of your key points, leading to a forceful conclusion, with an emotional appeal as the lasting impression.

3. *ELOCUTIO* (style)

This is all about making your audience want to listen to your ideas and your argument. It is about how you do it—the way you come across.

Style is often described as the extraordinary use of language. It should be based in correctness, clarity and appropriateness but enlivened through ornament,— an unusual use of language.

Rhetorical questions, clever turns of phrase and surprising figures of speech are all part of this.

Above all, your style must be one that is just right for your audience. You must be seen to speak "their" language (see page 77).

4. *MEMORIA* (memory)

This is the process of learning and memorizing your speech so you can deliver it without the use of notes. As notepaper was rare, the ancient orators had to memorize their speeches as they held forth in the forum.

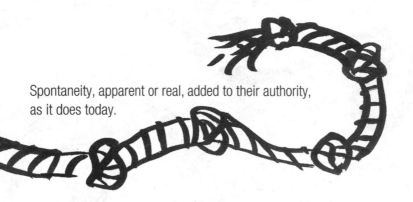

Spontaneity, apparent or real, added to their authority, as it does today.

Rather than memorizing or reading from a script, the best "spontaneous" solution is to prepare notes to refer to. Assuming you have a reasonable grasp of your content, these need only contain the key headings and signpost words that will keep you on track.

These same signposts, together with considered pauses, will help make you more memorable to your audience, the other aspect of *memoria.*

5. *ACTIO* (delivery)

Apparently when Cicero finished speaking, the people said, "How well he spoke," but when Demosthenes finished they said, "Let's march!"

When asked what was the most important component in oratory, Demosthenes replied **"DELIVERY."** Asked what was second, he responded, **"DELIVERY"** and third, **"DELIVERY."**

PREPAR

ATION.

"DISCOVER THE BEST AVAILABLE MEANS OF PERSUASION."

ARISTOTLE

DO YOUR HOMEWORK

Preparing for any live performance calls for multitasking. You're your own scriptwriter, actor, stage manager, choreographer, director, producer and . . . researcher.

In this latter role, you must explore everything that just might prove useful. Consider everything related to this particular audience, at this time, in this place and on this occasion.

Typically the less experienced jump to a solution, usually the most predictable one, before they have assembled a wealth of insights to play with. And, once you start along a chosen path, it is difficult to change to a more interesting route.

Give researcher-you some time! Time to look for different approaches and to think outside the box.

"If I had an hour to solve a problem, I'd spend 55 minutes thinking about the problem and 5 minutes thinking about solutions." **ALBERT EINSTEIN**

PUT YOURSELF IN THEIR SHOES

Everything starts with your understanding of your audience.

Who are they? Why are they here? What do they want?

Some answers will be obvious and others can be researched,
but the last question demands—and often doesn't get—serious thought
and intelligent guesswork.

To do this you must put yourself in their shoes.

Are they going to learn something new that will be useful or help their
decision? Will their problem get solved? Will the solution promised be
different or unexpected?

What is in it for them? Will they feel reassured, excited, optimistic,
positive or moved?

Note the personal nature of the questions. The closer you can
tune in to your audience's wavelength, the more impact you will
make on them.

*"It is not that I'm so smart. But I stay with the questions
much longer."* **ALBERT EINSTEIN**

IF YOU WANT TO BE HEARD, LISTEN

When getting ready to face an audience, perhaps for the first time, it is easy to fall into the trap of trying too hard to make your point, telling them what you want to say rather than what they might want to hear.

Two of Britain's finest interviewer-broadcasters were David Frost and Alan Whicker. They shared the characteristic of being superb listeners. They enabled their interviewees to talk, guards down, resulting in riveting and revealing two-way communication.

People listen to you if you listen to them.

"Knowledge speaks, but wisdom listens."
JIMI HENDRIX

YOU CRAM THESE WORDS INTO MY EARS AGAINST THE STOMACH OF MY SENSE.

WILLIAM SHAKESPEARE

50 WORDS
TO WOO YOUR LOVER

You should be able to condense your whole story or speech to 50 persuasive words—words that capture the hearts, not just the minds, of your audience. This is sometimes called the "elevator pitch."

Even if you are going to talk or present for an hour or more, the essence needs to be captured in order to set up what you will develop and embellish later on.

Creating a quick pitch or summary not only clarifies your own thinking, but it lets your audience know what's in store, whets their appetite and reinforces their understanding of your message and why it is important to them.

Here are my 32 words:

Based on the experience of 1,000 pitches, this book Contains a Constant source of ideas and inspiration to help you perform at your BEST and be a WINNER when it really matters.

Shopping List

apples   yogurt
other fruit   frozen peas
some berries   fish fingers
King Edwards   ice cream
ginger   apple juice
garlic   wine
noodles   brown bread
beansprouts   rolls
bacon   plain flour
salmon   raisins
sausages   Coke
ham
cheddar
S...ps × 3   cling film
butter   shampoo
MILK   toothpaste
                      light bulbs

OMNE TRIUM PERFECTUM: THE USEFUL RULE OF THREE

Lists have their place: often on a fridge door, as a reminder of what to do or what to buy. Lists do not have a place when you want to communicate with your audience.

You may have 20 burning issues to get across, but no matter how brilliantly you express them, the audience won't easily take them in if you do not have a simple structure that guides their listening.

To make life easier for them, you need to arrange, or group, your argument into no more than three themes or areas that support your subject. So **"BURNING ISSUES"** can be arranged into **"HOT," "RED HOT"** and **"FLAMING."**

Each of these themes can be separately developed, but with no more than three supporting points.

Use the rule-of-three blueprint on the following page to plot your next performance in front of an audience.

RULE-OF-THREE BLUEPRINT

OPENING REMARKS ——

SUBJECT/PROPOSITION ——

(UP TO) THREE THEMES ——

THEME CONCLUSIONS ——

OVERALL CONCLUSION ——

EMOTIONAL CLOSE ——

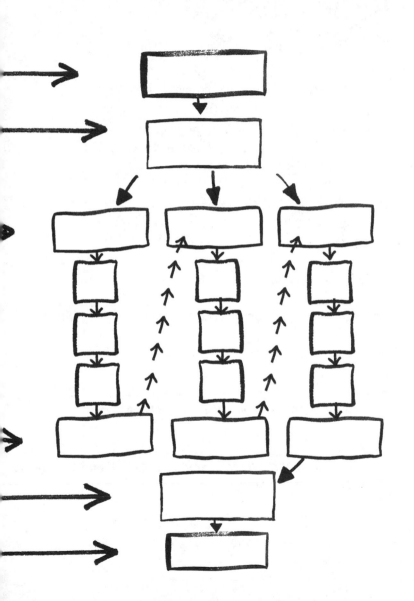

SPEECH STRUCTURE DEMONSTRATION

Follow this simple structure to arrange content that can be delivered with confidence and clarity. (The typed words below represent a notional script; the handwritten words are your "performance" reminders.) Try reading it aloud and then create your own using similar reminders.

(OPEN TO CONNECT, EASILY, WITH AUDIENCE)

"Good morning!" *Looking up, smiling,* **PAUSE**

"My name is Michael Parker." *Looking up, smiling,* **PAUSE**

"It is great to see so many golf lovers here today." *Smile,* **PAUSE**

(UPPING THE EMOTIONAL TEMPO)

"Today I am talking about golf and sharing with you my views on why more people should start playing this greatest of games!"
PAUSE

"To do this I will look at the three characteristics that make the game so special to all of us." **PAUSE**

"The first is the unique nature of the game" **PAUSE**
"then, the delight of being outdoors" **PAUSE** **"and finally, the social aspect"** **PAUSE**

44

It is the PAUSES that will make you seem confident and allow the audience to keep up. Signposting your key themes (see page 110) will help you memorize your speech and help your audience follow it.

(THE REASONS WHY)

"Taking the unique nature first . . ." PAUSE
– Expand on this using no more than three supports to this point, then summarize and PAUSE

"Now let's look at the outdoor delights . . ." PAUSE
– Expand on outdoor delights with up to three points . . . PAUSE summarize . . . PAUSE

"Finally we have the unique social aspect . . ." PAUSE
– Elaborate with, at most, three supports . . . PAUSE summarize . . . PAUSE

(FROM REASON TO EMOTIONAL HIGH)

"In conclusion . . ."
– Briefly remind how nature, the outdoors and the social side make golf the "greatest" . . . PAUSE and finish powerfully . . .

"How can anyone in their right mind resist taking up golf?"

TIME
DOTH FLIT;

oh shit!

Dorothy Parker

TO COME FIRST, DON'T ACT LAST-MINUTE

Give yourself time to prepare.

Of course, any pitch situation is about the adrenaline rush and the thrill of the occasion, but too often we leave things to the very last minute.

If you do, you run the risk that when the big day arrives you will be rushed and feel out of control, adding to any nerves you may suffer.

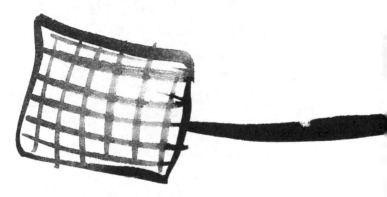

On day one, the moment you know a "performance" is coming up, think of your strategy, draw up a plan of attack and act on it.

The earlier your preparation, the sooner your rehearsal, and the more you will be relaxed, confident and . . . a winner.

PRODUCTIVITY

Morning

ENERGY:
THE PREMIUM FUEL
(top up in the morning)

Energy is infectious. Your audience will feed off it and return it. Everyone is lifted. Without it they will feel flat and so will you.

You face what may be a once-in-a-lifetime opportunity and only you at your most energetic best will do. Avoid falling into the noble trap of adding the intense demands of preparation to a tough daily routine. Set priorities to favor showtime!

Aim to benefit from the concept of "morning energy." Most individuals, and all teams, are at their freshest early on. This applies to audiences too, so always try to pitch earlier rather than later.

"Energy. It's 75% of the job. If you haven't got it, be nice."
PAUL ARDEN

Noon   evening

TIME FOR PLAIN SPEAKING

Often when we start writing a speech or preparing an interview response, we use different language from our everyday speech, and it ends up sounding formal, pompous or stilted when spoken out loud.

The secret is that your speech should sound like you, but polished. Use plain English when expressing your thoughts and ideas. Think of it as animated conversation.

Whether you choose to read your speech (if you absolutely have to), speak from your notes (see page 113) or, best of all, talk from memory using signposts (see page 110), speak plainly.

Keep your sentences short. That will make them punchy and memorable.

Perhaps record yourself to hear what you sound like. Do the words you've used trip off the tongue? Do you feel comfortable saying them? Do they sound like you?

Rehearse till you feel confident.

The goal is to sound natural, unrehearsed, spontaneous even.

"Simplicity is the ultimate sophistication."
LEONARDO DA VINCI

VISUAL AIDS ARE ONLY A GOOD IDEA IF THEY HAVE A GOOD IDEA

Charts, PowerPoint, props, videos and Twitter feeds can all play a part in enhancing the audience's enjoyment and understanding. This does not mean you should use them.

Only use them if they make for better communication—for a particular audience, in a particular venue. They are the icing on the cake, not the cake.

Don't start with an automatic assumption that you will need 20 PowerPoint charts. Start with your proposition and structure, write the basic content, then, and only then, use your imagination to search for props and visuals—ideas—that add meaning, surprise, drama or memorability.

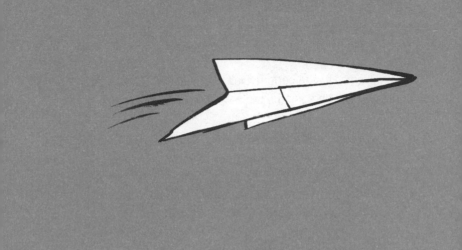

FAIL TO REHEARSE, PREPARE TO FAIL

Most will agree that to perform well you must rehearse, and yet most will put it off. Why? Here are the five common excuses:

- "I ran out of time." **Make time. Make rehearsal a deadline, not an option.**

- "The script needs revising." **An okay script properly rehearsed will outperform the "perfect" one unrehearsed.**

- "The visuals aren't ready." **You are more important. Rehearse without them.**

- "I like to reserve my energy." **You're avoiding the discomfort of rehearsal.**

- "Spontaneity will suffer." **The more rehearsed, the more confident you'll be. This enables spontaneity.**

Most of the excuses are a way of saying: "I can't face it." So, you must "feel the fear" and rehearse anyway.

When artist Grayson Perry delivered his Reith Lectures, he impressed with his engaging and, apparently, off-the-cuff approach. Broadcaster Sue Lawley, as she introduced him, said:

"He is one of the few lecturers to meet the agreed deadlines for delivery of the text, and the only one, to my knowledge, to ask for a full rehearsal."

FIND SOMEONE NEUTRAL TO JUDGE YOUR REHEARSAL (i.e., not your partner)

Whenever you are in the spotlight, you need to perform. This calls for rehearsal. This is not the same as a run-through, where you check all the practical things—timings, props, equipment, sitting, standing, handovers, staging and so on.

Rehearsal is all about what the audience takes out, not what you put in.

This means you need an audience, someone you trust, whose main role is not to criticize content but to encourage you, boost your confidence and tell you how you came across.

Ask your audience: Is my body language okay? How is my voice level? Am I pausing enough, maintaining my energy level, looking up, making eye contact?

What about memorable moments? Were there any dreary bits? Only master-of-suspense Alfred Hitchcock could get away with saying:

"Always make the audience suffer as much as possible."

Your audience should enjoy your performance. So should you.

YOUR CONCLUSION: THE ONLY WAY IS UP

Amelia Earhart, the first woman to fly solo across the Atlantic, said:

"It is far easier to start something than it is to finish it."

This is true of many performances in front of an audience.

Rehearsals typically focus on the start of a speech, not the conclusion. On the day, some people don't pace themselves properly and run out of steam. Or they can't wait to get off the "stage" and fail to make the final impression a lasting one.

Your conclusion is the opportunity to reinforce your key message, and to appeal to the mind.

Most of all, it is the opportunity to let go, take a risk, finish on a high note and aim for the heart.

"End with a bang, not a whimper." MODERN PROVERB

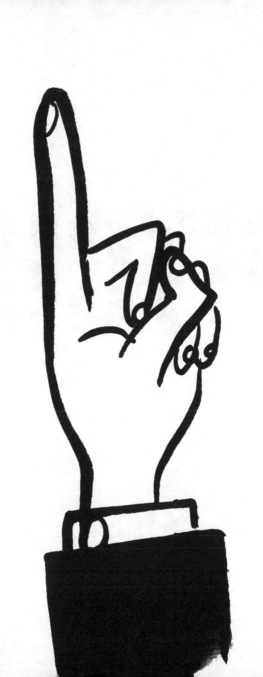

PITCH.

"NEVER VENTURE, NEVER WIN."

SUN TZU, THE ART OF WAR

FIRST IMPRESSIONS COUNT

One, two, three, four, five, six, seven seconds . . . or less.

That's how long we take to size up people on the first meeting.
It's instinctive, governed by our gut reaction to body language,
expression and tone of voice.

So consider how you come into the room, how you walk, shake hands,
stand or sit down, smile (please) and speak your first words ("hello" or
"good evening"). It's worth practicing your entrance—one, two, three,
four, five, six, seven times.

First impressions are instantly formed and will influence all that follows.

"You never get a second chance to make a first impression."
SOURCE UNKNOWN

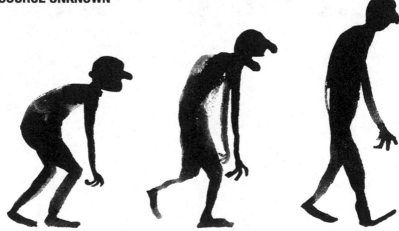

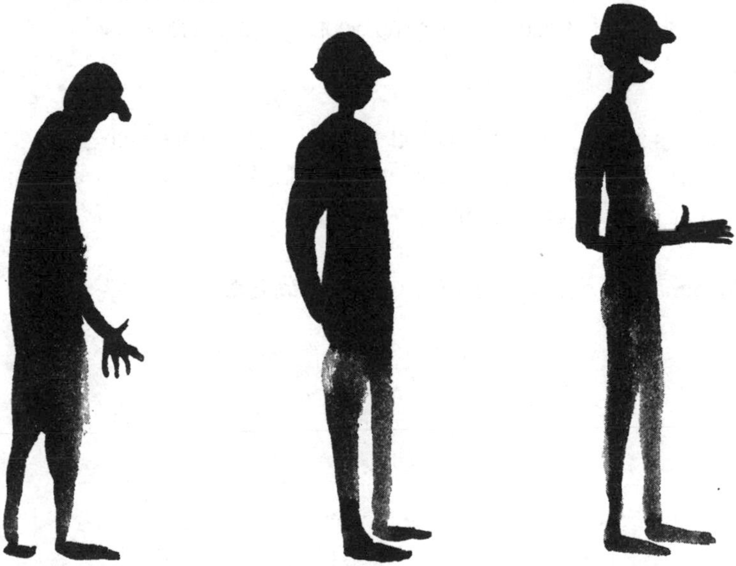

A WINNING START MEANS A WINNING FINISH

You may have been given 20 or more minutes to make your case, deliver a speech or argue for funds. This does not mean your audience will wait until you've finished before making up their minds. They will often reach their conclusions well before you've reached the end.

The vital first impression, in the first few seconds, raises expectations. The next few minutes should fulfil them.

This is when you set out your stall, introducing yourself. You start with your proposition, the "50 words to woo your lover" (see page 38), and then present the agenda you'll be following: your three supporting points (see page 41).

Doing this with clarity, authority and zest will reassure and relax your audience. They will know where you are coming from and where you are going. And they will already be more than halfway to their decision.

"The secret of getting ahead is getting started."
MARK TWAIN

TO INSPIRE OTHERS, YOU NEED TO BE INSPIRED

The *Oxford English Dictionary* describes the outcomes of being ***inspiring***:

to arouse a feeling: ***inspire confidence in others.***
to influence or compel: ***inspire to greater efforts.***
to animate or invigorate: ***inspire a specific action.***

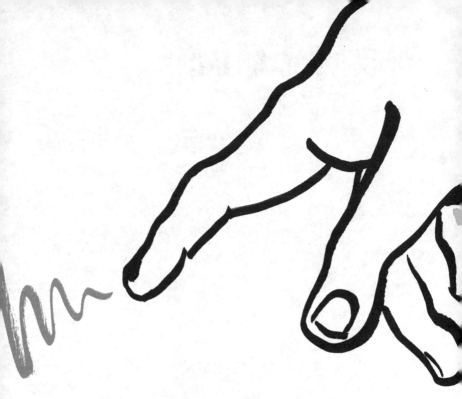

You may not be Martin Luther King Jr., but you can still be inspiring, provided you find something in your words that *fires you*. This can be a strongly held belief, excitement at discovering a new solution or a story not told before.

Whatever your fuel might be, grab hold of it and use it to inspire you; the rest will follow.

"One child, one teacher, one book, one pen can change the world." **MALALA YOUSAFZAI**

ONCE UPON A TIME . . .

TELL THEM A STORY

Nothing is as powerful in a pitch as a good story. Booker Prize–winning writer A.S. Byatt said: ***"Narration is as much part of human nature as breath and the circulation of the blood."***

In his mesmerizing election victory speech in Chicago, President Obama told this story:

"This election had many firsts and many stories that will be told for generations. But one that's on my mind tonight is about a woman who cast her ballot in Atlanta. She's a lot like the millions of others who stood in line to make their voice heard in this election except for one thing: Ann Nixon Cooper is 106 years old.

"She was born just a generation past slavery; a time when there were no cars on the road or planes in the sky; when someone like her couldn't vote for two reasons—because she was a woman and because of the color of her skin."

He developed this story to bring alive the promise he was making to the American people.

"She was there for the buses in Montgomery, the hoses in Birmingham, a bridge in Selma, and a preacher from Atlanta who told a people that 'We shall overcome.'

"Yes we can."

From childhood we have enjoyed and engaged with stories. We love them. We remember them. If you want to tap into emotion, find a story that connects, illuminates and engages.

LEARN FROM THE GREEKS

Over 2,000 years ago, Aristotle identified the three appeals, or "proofs," that are at the heart of persuasive speaking.

- ***Ethos*** is the appeal from the character of the speaker.

- ***Logos*** is the appeal based on rational argument.

- ***Pathos*** is the appeal to the emotions of the audience.

Without thinking, we use all three in everyday conversation when we are making a point. When faced with preparing something formal, we tend to focus only on reason, *logos*, assuming that *pathos* will occur naturally, and often overlooking *ethos* altogether.

It's essential to consider how these three appeals work together to arrive at the most compelling and persuasive argument.

"The whole is greater than the sum of its parts." **ARISTOTLE**

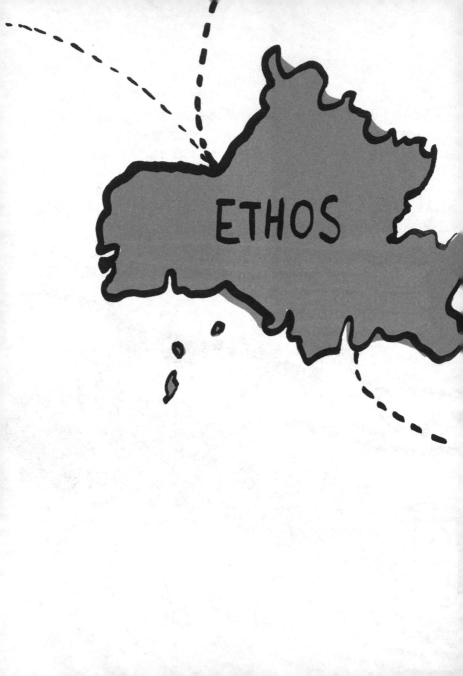

If your audience doesn't feel that you are one of them, speaking their language and therefore worth hearing, they won't listen. No matter how brilliant you are.

Establishing a bond, a rapport, between you and your audience in the opening minutes is essential.

You can achieve this through your appearance, body language and, not least, eye contact and handshake (where appropriate) as you make your entrance. Then your introductory remarks, before you launch into your subject, should provide an insight into a shared interest, a common ground.

Your audience can then relax.
You are on their side.

The manner of your introduction should be intimate rather than distant, closing the gap between you and your audience. You should lean forward if seated and, when standing, move toward them.

"Ich bin ein Berliner!"
PRESIDENT KENNEDY, 1963, WEST BERLIN

Logos is at the heart of a well-written essay. But for the live audience, the way the information is received is quite different.

Readers can reflect, ponder, pause or go back to check for meaning at their own pace. The live audience has no such option. If they miss a step in your logic, they can't press pause or replay.

When you're live, you need greater simplicity, clarity of expression and an unmistakeable flow to your reasoning. There should be no lengthy, complicated paragraphs. Instead, there should be lots of common sense, plus some examples. And maybe you can use a maxim (a pithy statement that speaks little but does much) to illustrate your thinking.

In preparation, make sure your basic premise and support are unarguable, then reinforce with the emotional arsenal.

"Don't raise your voice. Improve your argument."
ARCHBISHOP DESMOND TUTU

Logos will set the scene for consideration, but it is emotion that will lead to action. And it's not just any old emotion; you will, or should, have identified a shared feeling with your audience (*pathos*) as the focus of your appeal.

This may be anger, outrage or fear; optimism, excitement or pride . . .

Vivid, compelling language should be used to capture the audience emotionally—with words and images that evoke the desired feelings.

A story, or anecdote, that dramatizes your issue is often the most powerful way of swaying your audience and triggering their emotional response.

Then it's the passionate nature of your delivery: the *way* you say it. To rouse your audience, let them feel your feelings.

"Thou canst not speak of that thou dost not feel."
WILLIAM SHAKESPEARE, *ROMEO AND JULIET*

THE LONGER YOU GO ON, THE LESS THE IMPACT

Abraham Lincoln's Gettysburg Address, the most famous speech in American history, had:

272 words

and lasted less than:

3 minutes.

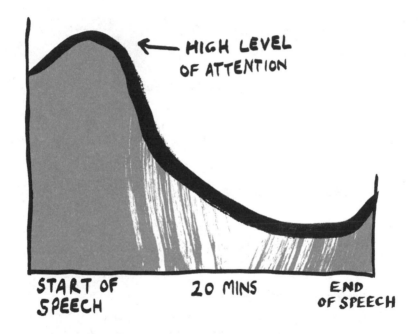

Things to consider: Everyone's attention span is declining.
People are possibly social networking while you're talking.
A TED talk is 18 minutes long.
Speed dating is 5 minutes long.

QUESTIONS &

How important is a Q & A session to decision makers?

How much time should be given to the session?

Can you prepare for unknown questions?

Will my résumé or advance document have been read?

Do I address my answer to the panel or the individual questioner?

What is the secret to a good answer?

How much detail should I go into?

How should a team handle questions?

Is it worth rehearsing, as questions are not known?

How can I finish strongly?

ANSWERS

It's all important in an interview, but can be just as important after a pitch.

Where you have control, never let the formal presentation eat into question time.

You can anticipate 80% of the subject area.

Perhaps. In an average panel, less than 50% will have read it.

Focus on, and flatter, the questioner at the start and finish. But don't ignore the others.

Your manner and the way you answer give the essential clues to your personality and attitude.

Avoid the long answer. Judgment will be based more on your initial response.

The team leader fields and passes a question to a team member. Avoid multiple answering.

Yes! You are still on stage, in performance mode.

Be ready with a brief thank-you. End on a positive note.

THE DREADED PANEL INTERVIEW: SOME DOS AND DON'TS

Aspects of psychographic profiling, which can measure personality traits, may sometimes be used before mega pitches, in jury selection or by recruiters. Most interviewees, however, will only meet their audience for the first time on the day.

You're going in blind in terms of the personalities facing you, so you must rely on your instincts to handle three main responses:

NICE, **NEUTRAL** and **NASTY**.

The majority of interviewers will be nice, interested in you, wanting you to do well. They put you at ease and they listen. This makes your task easier. Engage with them, enjoy the encounter, take the risks and go for it. But don't let Nice trap you into going off track and talking too much.

Neutrals may be reluctant participants or may be attentive but prefer not to show it. The resulting lack of interest, actual or apparent, is disconcerting. Don't overcompensate. Don't strive to get a reaction.

Nasties want to be the center of attention and exert authority with tough questions, and some may be role-playing. Don't get defensive, and definitely avoid confrontation. Don't be rushed into a response.

Do stay calm. Be concise, positive and honest. Maintain your overall composure. Assertion, not aggression, is key.

Remember

GIVE THEM SOMETHING TO REMEMBER YOU BY

You gave a well-prepared speech or a convincing case for selection, or you were just being your charming best. But will you be remembered?

A few hours or days or weeks later, how will they remember you after the many more interviews and presentations they see?

If you are totally brilliant, then you may be remembered for everything you said. This is unlikely. Most of us have to settle for less. Make sure that—at the very least—something stays in the mind. So take the **Memorable Test**.

If you can't put a big check mark next to one of these, you will quickly be forgotten:

A compelling story ☐

A repeatable phrase ☐

A piece of pure theater ☐

An unlikely setting ☐

An astounding visual ☐

Audience participation ☐

Best of all, an idea! ☐

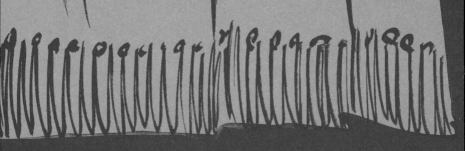

LIGHTS, CAMERA . . . ACTION!

It's showtime. Time to find the actor in you and bring a sense of the theater to what you do.

Think of the memorable performances of Winston Churchill on the radio, Martin Luther King Jr. at the Lincoln Memorial or Steve Jobs introducing the iPhone.

Your stage may not be on the steps of the Lincoln Memorial, but whether your audience is a solitary dry interviewer or a boisterous wedding party, you are performing. Whether you like it or not, you're on stage. You need to find your own touch of theater.

The words you have prepared must be turned into an **experience**.

Imagination and staging can add pizzazz. Consider movement and gesture, a dramatic entrance, a compelling story told with feeling, elements of surprise, props that add flavor or intrigue, an unexpected setting and, not least, tone of voice.

Just as an actor takes time to get into a part, so should you. With rehearsal you will become more natural on stage and more spontaneous, creating an interesting, engaging experience.

"Drama is life with the dull bits cut out." **ALFRED HITCHCOCK**

PERFOR

MANCE.

"IF TRUTH WERE SELF-EVIDENT, ELOQUENCE WOULD BE UNNECESSARY."

CICERO

Even the Pope gets nervous. Here are five helpful steps:

1. **Break your speech down** into less-daunting bite-size chunks—each no more than, say, two to four minutes—and deliver them as if they were separate mini-speeches.

2. **Conquer your opening.** Your first words are the scariest. Make them short, easy to say, easy to remember, easy to listen to. There should be nothing too clever and no jokes.

3. **Memorize your signposts** (the key words that signal each main thought) using the rule of three (see page 41). They will keep you on track and reduce the need for notes.

4. **Rehearse to someone neutral** (performing, not just reading). The more you rehearse, the less nervous you will be. If you rehearse alone, do it out loud, to the mirror.

5. **Practice the pauses** most of all. Pause to breathe deeply. Pause for thought. Pauses will make you *appear* confident and they *help* your confidence.

"PITCHES HAPPEN IN THE PAUSES."

CAROLINE GOYDER

Whether you are talking on the phone, at an interview or at a presentation, the easiest thing you can do to bolster your confidence and improve your communication is to . . .

PAUSE.

This does not call for changing your speed of speech, which is tough to do. It is simply practicing what we all do naturally in everyday conversation—when we pause for thought, pause to check we are understood and pause for emphasis. Even nervous gabblers can come across as confident if they . . .

PAUSE.

In music, as Claude Debussy said, *"Music is the space between the notes."* And pianist Artur Schnabel claimed: *"The notes I handle no better than many pianists. But the pauses between the notes—ah, that is where art resides."*

For many, particularly the less experienced, mastering the pause is the easiest, and quickest, route to better spoken communication. And the pause is not new. Here is how it was explained to students in ancient Rome:

"Pauses strengthen the voice. They also render the thoughts more clear-cut by separating them, and leave the hearer time to think."
AUTHOR UNKNOWN, *AD HERENNIUM*

LET'S FACE IT, ALL PERFORMANCES CARRY RISK

Whether you're an experienced concert pianist or a novice speaker, any performance has an element of risk. Even for runner Usain Bolt—whose false start cost him a world title. It's part of the thrill for the audience. It is, or should be, part of the excitement for you, the performer, too.

Basically there are two ways of facing risk. One is to worry like hell, and dwell on Murphy's Law (that anything that can go wrong will go wrong).

The other is to recognize and embrace the risks, confident in your ability to rise to the occasion.

Work carried out by Professor Aaron Williamon, head of performance science at the Royal College of Music in London, shows that this ability can be reinforced by **mastering the experience** of performance through replicating it as closely as possible in the lead-up.

Once you are familiar with your material, move to practicing alone (aloud, in front of a mirror), to rehearsal in front of people, to your "stage" performance. As you face the varying degrees of risk, you become more comfortable with it.

TALK FROM THE HEART, NOT THE CHART

It's all too easy to let the charts do the talking and become center stage.

As stated earlier, visual aids are valuable if they have ideas that add clarity or impact (see page 52), but, however compelling they may be, they're not as essential to the communication as *you*.

Your audience is infinitely more interested in you, so don't become a slave to the words shown. And definitely resist reading aloud from them.

Memorize your charts and rehearse them so they are a springboard for you to perform with spontaneity and emotion.

And, if the charts don't add something, chuck them.

"When the heart speaks, the mind finds it indecent to object."
MILAN KUNDERA, *THE UNBEARABLE LIGHTNESS OF BEING*

WITHOUT SIGNPOSTS, YOU'RE LOST

Think of your speech or presentation as a journey for you (the driver) and your audience (the passengers), and your overriding proposition is your destination.

To help your audience, and yourself, on the journey, it is essential to signal where you are and where you're going. You do this by giving them signposts to your three supporting themes.

Signal these key themes, with pauses to add emphasis, at the start and the conclusion of each phase of the journey.

The longer the journey, and the larger the audience, the more likely it is for people to be distracted and for their attention to wander. Once this happens you have lost them!

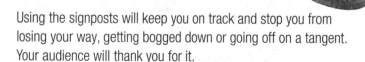

Using the signposts will keep you on track and stop you from losing your way, getting bogged down or going off on a tangent. Your audience will thank you for it.

READING

EA

DING

IS BAD

FOR THE EYES

Reading a speech is perfectly okay on the radio. A viewing audience, however, expects eye contact.

In normal conversation, we don't fix and hold a laser-like stare, daring our audience to flinch. What we do is catch their eye as we start, to check that they're with us. We then may glance away from time to time—gathering breath, pausing, pointing—but at the end of each thought, we check for connection before continuing.

If you are going to deliver a speech from a full script or notes, you should ape this pattern. You look up at the start of each sentence, checking for attention, and you must look up at the end (checking interest), reading as necessary in the middle.

Watch President Obama speaking from notes.

If you practice enough, your audience won't register that you're reading. But if you don't look up (as if dismissing them), they won't hear you.

"LOOK YOUR BEST— WHO SAID LOVE IS BLIND?"

MAE WEST

If we want to impress someone important—guest, lover, client, in-law—we want to look our best. At least, we'll give a quick glance in the mirror.

In most pitches, interviews and courtships, assume you have rivals almost as good-looking as you. If they take more trouble over their appearance than you, then they may get an advantage.

It could be wrong, it could be right, but the reality is, looks do influence judgment.

Pitches are won by inches, not miles, so leave nothing to chance.

The cheapest accessory is a smile!

"It's kind of like being on a date." **ROGER STERLING, *MAD MEN***

THE SERIOUS MATTER OF HUMOR

"I say, I say, I say, a funny thing happened to me on the way to . . ." is the classic opening of the old-time end-of-pier comic, and sometimes it was funny.

Unless you're a natural stand-up comedian, and very few are, don't even *try* to be funny. Telling jokes that work is an art form. Telling jokes that don't work is embarrassing to you and your audience.

Don't force humor; let it come out of the situation by being surprising, by coming up with startling facts, by telling interesting true stories, by revealing unexpected truths, by being charming and by showing your delight in your subject.

Don't try to be the next Woody Allen:

"If you want to make God laugh, tell him about your plans."

BECOME A POSEUR— YOU KNOW YOU'VE ALWAYS WANTED TO

When you're on stage, you'll be judged by your body language.

Given that there are, apparently, some 700,000 different signs, deciding which to adopt could be daunting.

Fortunately, you don't need to. Instead, remind yourself: if you have a song in your heart, you will walk with a spring in your step!

In other words, before your performance, decide the mood you want to feel in yourself (optimism, happiness, confidence, eagerness, bravado) and then practice the appropriate body language.

Walk with a swagger, enjoy filling your lungs, punch the air, keep your head high, your shoulders back, smile inanely in the mirror, take up a power pose. It works; try it now!

As social psychologist Amy Cuddy said in her brilliant TED talk:

"Fake it till you become it."

COMMAND YOUR STAGE

Like an actor, you're on stage from the second you start your presentation. Unlike an actor, you don't have a director telling you where to stand, when to sit, how to move and when to be still.

So be your own director.

Sit where the audience will sit—either for real or in your imagination. Direct the impression you can make by taking ownership of your stage, whether it is an interview chair or a platform.

Are the chairs too low or the lecterns too high? Are you the focus, not the screen? If you stand for authority, make sure you don't crowd their space. Think about how movement can add impact.

British Prime MInister David Cameron, bidding for leadership at his 2005 party conference, chose not to stand behind the lectern as his rivals did. Speaking without notes, he commanded the stage and was seen as a leader. The powerful Angela Merkel, the chancellor of Germany, will rearrange the chairs at a conference herself for better communication.

If she does this, shouldn't you?

wow!...

DID I JUST DO THAT?

Auditions, speeches and presentations all have in common the need to rise to the occasion—to perform at your best. However, this is not easy; it calls for an attitude and an approach that delights in the challenge.

Arguably the best approach ever was written in the 16th century by an Italian named Baldassare Castiglione. He identified two principles that, when working in balance, resulted in great performance.

The first of these is:

This covers all the hard work, preparation, studying, practicing of technique, methodology, refining and rehearsal. All of these are essential, and their combination will give a performance that is worthy—but it will not necessarily be inspired.

The second principle is:

sprezzatura

This word was coined by Castiglione and has variously been described as the vital spark, the flash of lightning, recklessness, the art of nonchalance, a touch of the ridiculous, rehearsed spontaneity, studied carelessness, practiced naturalness, joy in improvisation, embracing the unknown and enjoying it . . .

Rarely can the two have been so dramatically in evidence as on the biggest stage in sports, the Olympic Games. In London 2012, the eight fastest men in the world lined up on the start line for the 100 meters. They had each put in four years of dedication and training, *decoro*, preparing for this one race.

One man did more than rise to the occasion. The word *sprezzatura* might have been coined for Usain Bolt, the fastest man in the world, and, at that moment, its greatest performer.

JUST ONE LAST THING: BE YOURSELF—BUT BETTER

This is the standard well-meaning advice before you face a big life-changing meeting, but—like much advice—it is easier said than acted on.

All any "judge" wants to feel is that they've met the real, unvarnished, authentic, unique, interesting you. This should be easy, but the stakes are high. No one likes being judged. Natural expressions are inhibited. The occasion can overwhelm.

If you met the same individual or individuals in an informal nonjudgmental setting, the natural you would come into play spontaneously. With practice and rehearsal, your confidence will grow (as shown in the next section). Then your performance will gain a degree of prepared spontaneity so you will be seen at your best, or better!

"Be yourself; everyone else is already taken." **OSCAR WILDE**

PERFE

CT.

"TAKE PAINS; BE PERFECT."

WILLIAM SHAKESPEARE, A MIDSUMMER NIGHT'S DREAM

CONFIDENCE TRICKS

Stay calm. Be prepared.

Keep it simple. Less is more.

Play to your strengths.

Master your opening words.

Practice out loud.

Rehearse, rehearse, rehearse.

Rehearse before an audience.

Be comfortable with visual aids.

Get familiar with your venue.

Memorize your signposts.

Don't try to make jokes.

Storytelling comes naturally.

Walk tall to feel tall.

Pause . . . Pause . . . Pause.

Don't rush to answer questions.

Look the part to play the part.

Breathe deeply before you start.

Look up, not down.

Treat the audience as a friend.

Trust your instincts.

Oh ... and brush your teeth!

HOW LONDON WOOED
AND WON THE OLYMPICS

London's bid to host the 2012 Olympics was a winning pitch, but what made it perfect was ***the way*** the bid triumphed. To win they had to overcome two cities, Paris and Madrid, both more strongly favored.

An early and critical decision was to replace the original London bid leader, the American businesswoman Barbara Cassani, with Lord Coe. This was *ethos* writ large. A non-athlete would never be seen by the International Olympic Committee as one of them, but Coe was.

All bidding cities did their ***homework***, but London seemed to ***listen*** harder to experts from earlier bids and from the media. They understood better the IOC decision process by the 107 members. Many votes would be cast along national alignment, but there would be a vital core of "floating" voters to target.

Short-listed from their technical bids, five cities met the rational criteria of being able to deliver a successful event. The only way to convince the voters in London's favor would be to persuade them to *act on emotion*.

An exercise of putting themselves into the shoes of their judges gave London the necessary emotional insight. As vice chairman Alan Pascoe explained, "We kept asking ourselves on behalf of the IOC—what's in it for them?"

The answer was about making a difference, articulated in *less than 50 words*. "London's vision is to reach young people all around the world, to connect them with the inspirational power of the Games, so that they are inspired to choose sport."

This compelling promise was reinforced by London's tangible desire, their *hunger*, demonstrated by "ambassadors" like David Beckham and Sir Steven Redgrave but perhaps most tellingly by then Prime Minister Tony Blair.

The G8 summit prevented him from being at the presentation, but in the days before, he visited Singapore and met individually, for 30 minutes or so, with over 30 IOC members. He put his personal **passion** on the line. France's President Chirac remained aloof.

When it came to **showtime**, London created a **theatrical experience** which, while thrilling to TV viewers worldwide, had only one purpose: to engage emotionally with the IOC judges. In preparation, **failing to rehearse** was not an option, ten rehearsals being the norm.

A glittering cast, including Princess Anne, the mayor of London, a secretary of state, Olympic champion Denise Lewis, plus 30 children—the embodiment of the promise to inspire—rose to the occasion superbly. Months of painstaking effort, **decoro**, culminated in a performance of unforgettable **sprezzatura**.

Throughout, Lord Coe's *leadership* and his eloquence were central to the bid, but the most *memorable* moment, and arguably the most significant, was his *telling of a story*, a story that captured the essence of London's bid.

"When I was 12, I was marched into a large school hall with my classmates. We sat in front of an ancient black-and-white TV and watched grainy pictures from the Mexico Olympic Games . . . That day a window to a new world opened to me . . . I knew what I wanted to do, and what I wanted to be . . . Today I stand before you with those memories still fresh, still inspired by this great movement."

Many months after London won, Lord Coe was asked if there was one thing that he felt was at the heart of their success. His reply: *"It was all down to the emotional connection."*

SOME PERSUASIVE WRITERS

Stephen Bayley/Roger Mavity, *Life's a Pitch*

Sharon Crowley/Debra Hawhee, *Ancient Rhetorics for Contemporary Students*

Carmine Gallo, *Talk Like TED*

Caroline Goyder, *Gravitas*

David Kean, *How Not to Come Second*

Sam Leith, *You Talkin' to Me?*

DESIGN TEAM

The "way you say it" is central to the concept of this book. So the look and feel, together with the visual ideas, are all important.

My thanks to the hugely talented Jim Salter, an award-winning former art director at Saatchi & Saatchi, and illustrator Sandra Salter, a BAFTA nominee for her animation work. www.saltysanimation.co.uk

Notes

Derick Walker for his constant flow of ideas and insight; Roger Kennedy and Richard Myers for their wisdom; Amanda Lees, my guide to the pitfalls of publishing; Imogen Sage bringing the voice of an actor; Eliza for adding her creative magic; daughters Laura and Hannah for keeping me grounded; and Sam Jackson for her transformational editing.

Persuading

"SPEAKING"

COMMUNICATION

interviewing

Fundrai$ing

Engaging

addressing
influencing
PROMOTING
Performing
PITCHING

Michael Parker is one of the UK's most experienced pitch coaches, having taken part in over 1,000 pitches—many successful, some not, but he learned from both! Additionally, Michael has competed as a hurdler in two Olympics, so he knows what it takes to perform under pressure. He now brings this experience and his competitive instincts to coaching, ranging from one-on-one interviews to major public speeches. Visit his website at pitchcoach.co.uk.